Life's Little Insp

Secrets of living wisely and living well

by the author of *Footprints*
MARGARET FISHBACK POWERS

*Duane,
New Class New
Book.
Love and Prayers,
Luan
Feb. 97*

HarperCollins*PublishersLtd*

Published simultaneously in the U.K. by Marshall Pickering, an Imprint of HarperCollins Religious, part of HarperCollins Publishers: 1996

First Canadian edition: 1996

To Beverly Still, our dear friend who has been an encouragement throughout many years. May He continue to bless you.

Canadian Cataloguing in Publication Data

Powers, Margaret Fishback
    Life's little inspiration book II : the secrets of living wisely & living well

ISBN 0-00-638585-0

1. Devotional literature, Canadian (English).*
I. Title.

BV4832.2.P68 1996   242   C96-930737-3

96 97 98 99 HC 10 9 8 7 6 5 4 3 2 1

Printed and bound in the United States

INTRODUCTION

W ho'd have thought that when I wrote the poem "I Had a Dream," now known as *Footprints*, that Thanksgiving in Ontario over 30 years ago, I'd be writing the introduction for the *second* volume of thoughts, sayings and quotes that is *Life's Little Inspiration Book II*? I've been absolutely thrilled at the success of the first collection, *Life's Little Inspiration Book*, and I sincerely hope that you'll enjoy the mixture of "a bit of this and a bit of that" just as much.

It's an assortment of sayings, "one-liners" and quotes that have been chosen from the "scrapbook" of personal thoughts that my husband Paul and I have been collecting over the years. They reflect the good times and the bad times which we all go through, and many stem from the letters you've sent telling me how *Footprints* has been a source of comfort and encouragement to you.

It still amazes me how people have refused to let *Footprints* stay an "ordinary" poem – they've passed it on to their friends, written it in their Bibles and *lived* it just as I have, refusing to let die the hope it offers. I know that for many of you, *Footprints* has been a way of communicating God's love to others, and for that I feel truly blessed.

The knowledge that our Savior walks with us every day, and the realization that we can reach out and clasp this Rock of Ages has been uppermost in my thoughts while putting together this collection. May these lines, which hold so much food for thought, warm your heart with the love of God and inspire you to extend that love into the lives of those around you.

Margaret Fishback Powers
Author of the poem *Footprints* and the book *Footprints: The True Story Behind the Poem that Inspired Millions*.
British Columbia, Canada 1996

FOOTPRINTS

One night I dreamed a dream.
I was walking along the beach with my Lord.
Across the dark sky flashed scenes from my life.
For each scene, I noticed two sets of footprints in the sand,
one belonging to me and one to my Lord.
When the last scene of my life shot before me
I looked back at the footprints in the sand.
There was only one set of footprints.
I realized that this was at the lowest
and saddest times of my life.
This always bothered me
and I questioned the Lord
about my dilemma.

"Lord, you told me when I decided to follow You,
You would walk and talk with me all the way.
But I'm aware that during the most troublesome
times of my life there is only one set of footprints.
I just don't understand why, when I needed You most,
You leave me."
He whispered, "My precious child,
I love you and will never leave you
never, ever, during your trials and testings.
When you saw only one set of footprints
it was then that I carried you."

© 1964 Margaret Fishback Powers

God will only carry those who allow
Him to carry them.

*I the Lord have called thee in righteousness, and will hold
thine hand, and will keep thee ...*

ISAIAH 42:6

Faith unlocks the door to ultimate achievement.

... Keep alert, stand firm in your faith, be courageous, be strong.

1 CORINTHIANS 16:13

He who harbors a grudge will miss
the haven of happiness.

But I say to you that if you are angry with a brother
or a sister, you will be liable to judgment ...

MATTHEW 5:22

Man's littleness is expressed by the
presence of the stars.

See the highest stars, how lofty they are!

JOB 22:12

Happiness is where it is found,
but seldom where it is sought. *(J. Billings)*

*I turned my mind to know and to search out
and to see wisdom ...*

ECCLESIASTES 7:25

Defeat may serve as well as victory to shake
the soul and let the glory out.

*... thanks be to God, who gives us the victory through
our Lord Jesus Christ.*

1 CORINTHIANS 15:57

Even though you do the right thing,
do you do it in the right way?

*In all your ways acknowledge him,
and he will make straight your paths.*

PROVERBS 3:6

Our greatest glory is not in never falling,
but in rising every time we fall.

Humble yourselves before the Lord, and he will exalt you.

JAMES 4:10

If you love your friends,
learn when to leave them.

The heart of the wise teacheth his mouth,
and addeth learning to his lips.

PROVERBS 16:23

Learning how to bear inescapable sorrow
is not easily done.

... have unity of spirit, sympathy, love for one another,
a tender heart, and a humble mind.

1 PETER 3:8

In the matter of salvation, he who hesitates is lost!

... God proves his love for us in that while we still were sinners Christ died for us.

ROMANS 5:8

God's treasure house, the Bible, is only
unlocked by the golden key of meditation.

This book ... thou shalt meditate therein day and night ...

JOSHUA 1:8

Nature is an outstretched finger
pointing towards God!

O Lord, how manifold are your works!

PSALM 104:24

When Christ prepares the table for us it is always
a well-balanced meal. *(H. K. Barclay)*

*You prepare a table before me in the presence
of my enemies ... my cup overflows.*

PSALM 23:5

Salvation is free, but you have to ask for it.
(Paul L. Powers)

Ask, and it will be given you; search, and you will find ...

LUKE 11:9

Without encouragement, any one of us
can lose confidence.

*... the fruit of the Spirit is love, joy, peace, patience,
kindness, generosity ...*

GALATIANS 5:22

Before becoming an effective worker for the Lord,
take time to study The Manual.

I treasure your word in my heart, so that
I may not sin against you.

PSALM 119:11

Home – a place where the small are great,
and the great are small.

*Seek ye first the kingdom of God, and his righteousness;
and all these things shall be added unto you.*

MATTHEW 6:33

The name of Jesus may be a byword to the sinner,
but it is a password to Heaven for the saint.

" ... the Messiah ... Whose son is he?"
They said to him, "The son of David."

MATTHEW 22:42

You cannot whitewash yourself by
blackening others.

... and be kind to one another ... forgiving one another,
as God in Christ has forgiven you.

EPHESIANS 4:32

I can't see the pattern into which each
tangled thread is bent, but in trusting the Father,
I am content.

... for I have learned to be content with whatever I have.

PHILIPPIANS 4:11

In the Christian life, an ounce of truth
is worth a ton of talk.

Let the wise also hear and gain in learning ...

PROVERBS 1:5

A happy memory is the most valuable thing in the world. It's a hiding place for "unforgotten treasures."
(Paul L. Powers)

Take delight in the Lord, and he will give you the desires of your heart.

PSALM 37:4

Sooner or later, all of us come to a "Red Sea" place in life.

The Lord drove the sea back ... and turned it into dry land ...
The Israelites went into the sea on dry ground.

EXODUS 14:21–22

Don't just count your years, make your years count!
(Dr Ernest Meyers)

*I know that there is nothing better for them than to be happy
and enjoy themselves as long as they live ...*

ECCLESIASTES 3:12

An optimist is someone who thinks the
future is uncertain.

Teach me the way I should go, for to you I lift up my soul.

PSALM 143:8

The Lord seeks men and women who are not ashamed to be seen down on their knees in prayer.

Then he withdrew from them about a stone's throw, knelt down, and prayed ...

LUKE 22:41

God is more concerned about your response to the problem than He is in removing the problem.

My eyes are ever toward the Lord,
for he will pluck my feet out of the net.

PSALM 25:15

It's a wise parent who knows how to encourage
a child's hidden talent.

*... do not provoke your children to anger, but bring them up
in the discipline and instruction of the Lord.*

EPHESIANS 6:4

The answer always comes,
but often as not in ways you least expect.

*Call to me and I will answer you, and will tell you great
and hidden things that you have not known.*

JEREMIAH 33:3

LIFE – Warning: hazardous journey ahead.
Be prepared for detours. *(Paul L. Powers)*

*Do not enter the path of the wicked,
and do not walk in the path of evildoers.*

PROVERBS 4:14

Other books were given for information;
the Bible was given for transformation.

*... be transformed by the renewing of your minds, so that you
may discern what is the will of God ...*

ROMANS 12:2

The most overloaded, desperate people, are those
who can see no other burdens but their own.

Bear one another's burdens,
and in this way you will fulfil the law of Christ.

GALATIANS 6:2

The character you end life with will be the
character you begin eternity with.

*For God hath not appointed us to wrath,
but to obtain salvation by our Lord Jesus Christ.*

1 THESSALONIANS 5:9

The whole secret of prolonging one's life consists in doing nothing to shorten it.

For once you were darkness, but now in the Lord you are light. Live as children of light ...

EPHESIANS 5:8

A best friend is someone who is in your corner
when you are cornered.

... *a true friend sticks closer than one's nearest kin.*
PROVERBS 18:24

Temptation is something you can't use
at a price you can't resist.

And lead us not into temptation, but deliver us from evil.

MATTHEW 6:13

A mistake a lot of preachers make is to think that they've been anointed, not appointed.

For this gospel I was appointed a herald
and an apostle and a teacher.

2 TIMOTHY 1:11

Confidence is the feeling that you have before you
really understand the problem.

*The wise are cautious and turn away from evil, but the fool
throws off restraint and is careless.*

PROVERBS 14:16

The reason many people don't live within their income is because they don't consider that living.

For what will it profit them to gain the whole world and forfeit their life?

MARK 8:36

God allows us to be in darkness so
He can show us He is the Light.

The people who walked in darkness have seen a great light ...

ISAIAH 9:2B

If you want the world to take notice of you,
don't sell yourself short.

The laborer is worthy of his reward.

1 TIMOTHY 5:18

The only thing worse than growing old is being
denied the privilege.

Do not cast me off in the time of old age;
do not forsake me when my strength is spent.

PSALM 71:9

If poverty is a blessing in disguise,
then in many cases the disguise is perfect.

*... give me neither poverty nor riches;
feed me with the food that I need.*

PROVERBS 30:8

Life with Christ is an endless hope;
without Him a hopeless end.

*... God chose to make known how great ... are the riches of the
glory of this mystery, which is Christ in you, the hope of glory.*

COLOSSIANS 1:27

People are lonely because they build walls
instead of bridges.

Do not be far from me,
for trouble is near and there is no one to help.

PSALM 22:11

Man builds for a century;
the Christian builds for eternity.

*... this one thing I do: forgetting what lies behind
and straining forward to what lies ahead.*

PHILIPPIANS 3:13

Christ helps us to face the music,
even when we don't like the tune.

What time I am afraid, I will trust in thee.

PSALM 56:3

Kindness has converted more sinners than zeal,
eloquence or learning.

"How beautiful are the feet of those who bring good news!"

ROMANS 10:15

Lost time is never found again!
(Paul L. Powers)

For everything there is a season,
and a time for every matter under heaven ...

ECCLESIASTES 3:1

The first step to victory: recognize the enemy!
(Paul L. Powers)

*Put on the whole armor of God, so that you may be able
to stand against the wiles of the devil.*

EPHESIANS 6:11

Well done is better than well said.

Ye are my friends, if ye do whatsoever I command you.

JOHN 15:14

Where God guides, He provides!

" ... you will have treasure in heaven; then come, follow me."

MARK 10:21

Is your life a witness, with testimony true?
Could the world be won to Christ by what others
see in you? *(Paul L. Powers)*

*... let your light shine before others, so that they may see your
good works and give glory to your Father in heaven.*

MATTHEW 5:16

Instead of counting your troubles,
try adding up your blessings! *(Dr Geoffrey Still)*

*... who has blessed us in Christ with every spiritual blessing
in the heavenly places ...*

EPHESIANS 1:3

Trials should make us better – not bitter.

*And whosoever doth not bear his cross,
and come after me, cannot be my disciple.*

LUKE 14:27

Blessed is the soul who is too busy to worry during the day and too tired to worry at night.

Be still before the Lord, and wait patiently for him ...

PSALM 37:7

Child's prayer overheard at camp: "Dear Jesus, I'll come again, 'cos I like myself when I'm near you." *(Paul L. Powers)*

Whosoever therefore shall humble himself as this little child, the same is greatest in the kingdom of Heaven.

MATTHEW 18:4

Christ is well known for working three days
ahead of schedule. *(Paula Powers)*

*"I will destroy this temple ... and in three days
I will build another ... "*

MARK 14:58

A smooth sea never made a skilful sailor.

... be instant in season, out of season; reprove, rebuke, exhort with all longsuffering and doctrine.

2 TIMOTHY 4:2

God is too good to be unkind and
too wise to make mistakes.

O Lord, you have searched me and known me ...
and are acquainted with all my ways.

PSALM 139:1,3

Pray believing, have faith and then trust!
(Dr Ernest Meyers)

Trust in the Lord with all your heart ... In all your ways acknowledge Him ...

PROVERBS 3:5,6

Disappointment and sorrow come to all.
There is no new individual experience in life
– only parallel cases.

*For we ourselves were once foolish ... But when the goodness and
loving kindness of God our Savior appeared, he saved us ...*

Titus 3:3–5

You can only be ready to live if you are ready to die. *(John & Betty Stamm, martyred missionaries)*

Yes, we do have confidence, and we would rather be away from the body and at home with the Lord.

2 CORINTHIANS 5:8

In creation we see God's hand;
in redemption we see His heart.

...Christ Jesus ... gave himself to redeem all mankind.

1 TIMOTHY 2:6

God's grace: EVERYTHING for NOTHING,
when we don't deserve ANYTHING.

*... the Lord will give grace and glory: no good thing will he
withhold from them that walk uprightly.*

PSALM 84:11

Your greatest gift to others is a good example.
(Dr Geoffrey Still)

*... Christ also suffered for you, leaving you an example,
so that you should follow in his steps.*

1 PETER 2:21

Man needs more than a new start,
he needs a new heart.

I the Lord test the mind and search the heart ...

JEREMIAH 17:10

When walking through the "valley of shadows,"
remember, a shadow is cast by a Light.
(H. K. Barclay)

Even though I walk through the darkest valley, I fear no evil ...

PSALM 23:4

There is always an "I" in the middle of sIn.
(Paul L. Powers)

How many are my iniquities and my sins?

JOB 13:23

The problem with doing nothing is
you can't stop to take a rest.

*"Come away to a deserted place all by yourselves
and rest a while."*

MARK 6:31

When you meet temptation, keep to the right!

Pray that ye enter not into temptation.

LUKE 22:40

Today's seed brings tomorrow's harvest.

May those who sow in tears reap with shouts of joy.

PSALM 126:5

Never borrow sorrow from tomorrow.

Banish anxiety from your mind, and
put away pain from your body ...

ECCLESIASTES 11:10

Narrow minds and wide mouths bring trouble!
(Paul L. Powers)

*" ... let them keep their tongues from evil
and their lips from speaking deceit ... "*

1 PETER 3:10

Prayer cuts knots you can't untie!

May the Lord fulfil all your petitions.

PSALM 20:5

Would people rather see you coming or going?

... God will make you worthy of his call and will fulfil by his power every good resolve and work of faith ...

2 THESSALONIANS 1:11

You can't break God's promises by leaning on them!

Cast all your anxieties on him, because he cares for you.

1 PETER 5:7

If you plant weeds don't expect to grow flowers!

*The wicked worketh a deceitful work: but to him that soweth
righteousness shall be a sure reward.*

PROVERBS 11:18

God very often digs wells of joy with the
spade of sorrow.

He heals the brokenhearted, and binds up their wounds.

PSALM 147:3

Tell EVERYONE about the ONLY ONE who can save ANYONE!

*"I am the way, and the truth, and the life.
No one comes to the Father except through me."*

JOHN 14:6

Patience carries a lot of WAIT!

... so that you may not become sluggish, but imitators of those who through faith and patience inherit the promises.

HEBREWS 6:12

When it comes to prayer some people need a
FAITH lift. *(Paula Powers)*

... let us work for the good of all,
and especially for those of the family of faith.

GALATIANS 6:10

The fruit of the Christian is ripened in Sonshine!

*But grow in the grace and knowledge of
our Lord and Savior Jesus Christ.*

2 PETER 3:18

Prayer does not need proof, it needs practice.

What things soever ye desire, when ye pray,
believe that ye receive them, and ye shall have them.

MARK 11:24

Angry at another's faults? Count ten – of your own!

One who is slow to anger is better than the mighty ...

PROVERBS 16:32

Christ has a message for this MESS AGE.
(Dr Barry Moore)

*At that day ye shall know that I am in my Father,
and ye in me, and I in you.*

JOHN 14:20

Treasures in Heaven are laid up only as
treasures on earth are laid down.

For where your treasure is, there your heart will be also.

MATTHEW 6:21

Is your memory rusty because your Bible is dusty?

*With my whole heart I seek you; do not let
me stray from your commandments.*

PSALM 119:10

The Bible is the only book whose author is always present when it is read.

"I am the Alpha and the Omega," says the Lord God, who is and who was and who is to come, the Almighty.

REVELATIONS 1:8

You never get a second chance to
make a first impression. *(Paula Powers)*

Let your speech be always with grace, seasoned with salt ...
COLOSSIANS 4:6

The poorest man is he whose only wealth
is money. *(Dr Leroy Gager)*

*Keep your lives free from the love of money,
and be content with what you have ...*

HEBREWS 13:5

God has included you in His plans
– have you included Him in yours? *(Paul L. Powers)*

For surely I know the plans I have for you, says the Lord,
plans for your welfare and not for harm …

JEREMIAH 29:11

After all is said and done,
more is usually said than done!

For God will bring every deed into judgment, including every secret thing, whether good or evil.

ECCLESIASTES 12:14

Easy street is a blind alley.

There is a way that seems right to a person,
but its end is the way to death.

PROVERBS 14:12

Each cross, each trouble has its day
— then passes away.

... but they that seek the Lord shall not want any good thing.

PSALM 34:10

Praise does wonders for the sense of hearing.

But exhort one another daily ... lest any of you be hardened through the deceitfulness of sin.

HEBREWS 3:13

A clear conscience is often the sign of
a bad memory.

Depart from evil, and do good; seek peace, and pursue it.

PSALM 34:14

Surrounded by peace, no one is ever alone.

Keep on doing the things that you have learned ...
and seen in me, and the God of peace will be with you.

PHILIPPIANS 4:9

You don't stop laughing because you grow old
– you grow old because you stop laughing.

A cheerful heart is a good medicine ...

PROVERBS 17:22

A Godly home: a father's kingdom,
a mother's world, a child's paradise.

I came that they may have life, and have it abundantly.

JOHN 10:10

Beware of hypocrisy
– it is better to be one-sided than two-faced!

*So you also on the outside look righteous to others, but inside
you are full of hypocrisy and lawlessness.*

MATTHEW 23:28

Keep your light shining.
God will put it where it can be seen.

While you have the light, believe in the light, so that you may become children of light.

JOHN 12:36

SCARS for Christ today mean STARS
for Christ tomorrow!

*From now on, let no one make trouble for me; for I carry the
marks of Jesus branded on my body.*

GALATIANS 6:17

Man measures his deed;
God measures the intentions.

That ye might walk worthy of the Lord unto all pleasing,
being fruitful in every good work ...

COLOSSIANS 1:10

Witnessing for Christ is not getting into the MOOD but being in the MODE. *(Paula Powers)*

"Whom shall I send, and who will go for us?"
And I said "Here am I; send me!"

ISAIAH 6:8

We learn from experience. A man never wakes his
second baby just to see her smile.

*"I have acquired great wisdom ... my mind has had
great experience of wisdom and knowledge."*

ECCLESIASTES 1:16

The best bridge between despair and hope
is a good night's sleep.

*He shall enter into peace: they shall rest in their beds,
each one walking in his uprightness.*

ISAIAH 57:2

Keep your confidence in God and
He'll keep your cares. *(H. K. Barclay)*

*... for the Lord will be your confidence and will keep
your foot from being caught.*

PROVERBS 3:26

No service is fruitful, unless done in the
power of the Holy Spirit.

If we live in the Spirit, let us also walk in the Spirit.

GALATIANS 5:25

All God's testings have a purpose;
someday you will see the light.

But for now just put your trust in Him; walk by faith, not by sight. How lovely is your dwelling place, O Lord of hosts!

PSALM 84:1

Don't be so concerned about working for God that you overlook dwelling with God.

I pray that ... Christ may dwell in your hearts through faith, as you are being rooted and grounded in love.

EPHESIANS 3:16,17

A good Christian shows the way, knows the way
and goes the way.

*He will feed his flock like a shepherd; he will gather the lambs
in his arms ... and gently lead the mother sheep.*

ISAIAH 40:11

Remember that the sign on the door
to opportunity reads: PUSH.

*... that God would open unto us a door of utterance,
to speak the mystery of Christ ...*

COLOSSIANS 4:3

In going out into the world, we often carry our "grief case" to do the daily work of the Lord.

Rejoice with those who rejoice, weep with those who weep.

ROMANS 12:15

The age of understanding and acceptance comes to different people at different times.

Come now, and let us reason together, saith the Lord ...

ISAIAH 1:18

The powers of the soul are commensurate
with its needs.

*... what does the Lord require of you but to do justice,
and to love kindness ...*

MICAH 6:8

The Resurrection makes a difference
– the difference between life and death,
light and darkness, hope and despair.

*By his great mercy he has given us a new birth into a living
hope through the resurrection of Jesus Christ from the dead ...*

1 PETER 1:3

Don't let your fears about the next hundred
years discourage you from smiling now
– occasionally, anyhow.

... fear not, for I am with thee, and will bless thee ...

GENESIS 26:24

Once formed, the habit of prayer becomes
as natural as breathing.

*Then Jesus told them a parable about their need to pray
always and not to lose heart.*

LUKE 18:1

No enemy is so near that God is not nearer.

. . . in the shadows of your wings I will take refuge,
until the destroying storms pass by.

PSALM 57:1

Trust God to overcome your difficulties
– he has had many thousands of years' experience.

Jesus Christ is the same yesterday and today and forever.

HEBREWS 13:8

Turn to God for help in shaping your life
– by prayer he will bring peace to the humblest.

*Just like the clay in the potter's hand,
so are you in my hand, O house of Israel.*

JEREMIAH 18:6

Bored people are not the under-privileged
but the over-privileged.

*See the one who would not take refuge in God, but trusted in
abundant riches, and sought refuge in wealth.*

PSALM 52:7

Success in dealing with others is like
making rhubarb pie – use all the sweetener
you can, then double it!

Neither shall you bear false witness against your neighbour.

DEUTERONOMY 5:20

Prayer is: Thank-, Ask-, Listen-, Know-ing
– to God!

*"You are my God; give ear, O Lord, to the voice
of my supplications."*

PSALM 140:6

Faith is continuing to run, confident that you will get your "second wind."

Brothers and sisters, do not be weary in doing what is right.

2 THESSALONIANS 3:13

Sometimes we don't read the writing on the wall
because we can't see it properly.

*Now my eyes will be open and my ears attentive to the
prayer that is made in this place.*

2 CHRONICLES 7:15

A kick in the pants sends you further along in life
than a friendly handshake.

*All scripture is inspired by God and is useful for teaching,
for reproof, for correction, and for training in righteousness ...*

2 TIMOTHY 3:16

An honest salesperson is one who sells goods that don't come back, to customers who do.

... we are sure that we have a clear conscience, desiring to act honorably in all things.

HEBREWS 13:18

A modern woman is one who puts off today what
her husband can do on the weekend.

The heart of her husband trusts in her,
and he will have no lack of gain.

A true missionary is God's child in God's place, doing God's work in God's way – for God's glory!

... because we look not at what can be seen but at what cannot be seen; for what can be seen is temporary, but what cannot be seen is eternal.

2 CORINTHIANS 4:18

When church services are over, your service begins.

And every day in the temple and at home they did not cease to teach and proclaim Jesus as the Messiah.

ACTS 5:42

Put God first – be happy at last!

"My heart exults in the Lord;
my strength is exalted in my God."

1 SAMUEL 2:1

Does your walk live up to your talk?
(B. Harback)

*... though we stumble, we shall not fall headlong,
for the Lord holds us by the hand.*

PSALM 37:24

Most of us won't be content with our
lot in life until it's a lot more.

*Of course, there is great gain in godliness
combined with contentment ...*

Faith can never overdraw its account
in the bank of Heaven.

"Whoever is faithful in a very little is faithful also in much ... "

LUKE 16:10

Jesus Christ – the light that knows no power failure.
(Paul L. Powers)

"I am the light of the world. Whoever follows me will never walk in darkness but will have the light of life."

JOHN 8:12